Corny Jokes

Joe King

Abdo Kids Junior
is an Imprint of Abdo Kids
abdobooks.com

Abdo
ABDO KIDS JOKES
Kids

abdobooks.com

Published by Abdo Kids, a division of ABDO, P.O. Box 398166, Minneapolis, Minnesota 55439.

Printed in the United States of America, North Mankato, Minnesota.

052023

092023

THIS BOOK CONTAINS RECYCLED MATERIALS

Photo Credits: Getty Images, Shutterstock

Production Contributors: Teddy Borth, Jennie Forsberg, Grace Hansen

Design Contributors: Candice Keimig, Pakou Moua

Library of Congress Control Number: 2022946708

Publisher's Cataloging-in-Publication Data

Names: King, Joe, author.

Title: Corny jokes / by Joe King

Description: Minneapolis, Minnesota : Abdo Kids, 2024 | Series: Abdo kids jokes | Includes online resources and index.

Identifiers: ISBN 9781098266042 (lib. bdg.) | ISBN 9781098266745 (ebook) | ISBN 97810982[illegible] (Read-to-me ebook)

Subjects: LCSH: Jokes--Juvenile literature. | Wit and humor--Juvenile literature. | Humor--Juvenile literature.

Classification: DDC 818.6--dc23

Table of Contents

Corny Jokes

Spring is here!

I got so excited, I wet my plants!

What did the fast tomato say to the slow tomato?

Ketchup!

Why shouldn't you tell secrets in a cornfield?

There are too many ears!

Where do fruits go on vacation?

Pear-is!

What's a sad strawberry called?

A blueberry.

What does a band of berries do together?

They have a jam session.

Where do polar bears
keep their money?

In a snowbank.

What do cats wear
when they go to bed?

Paw-jamas!

What do you call a fish wearing a bow tie?

Sofishticated.

I look fintastic!

Why are frogs happy?

They eat whatever bugs them!

What did the firefly say to her BFF?

"You glow, girl!"

What kind of photos will you find on a tortoise’s phone?

Shellfies.

RIP boiling water.

You will be mist.

I was wondering why the baseball was getting bigger and bigger.

Then it hit me.

It's raining cats and dogs.

Be careful not to step in a poodle!

Want to hear a long joke?

Joooooooooooooooooke.

What did the drummer
call his twin daughters?

Anna One, Anna Two!

I don't trust those trees.
They seem kind of shady.
I'll be leafing now.

Why did the bike fall over?

It was two tired.

What did the janitor say when he jumped out of the closet?

"Supplies!"

What has 6 wheels and flies?

A garbage truck!

This joke stinks!

Why did the man sell
his vacuum?

All it was doing was collecting dust.

Why can't you trust stairs?

They're always up to something.

You have a hole in your sock!

How else could you get your foot into it?

Do you know why the chili has 239 beans?

Because one more would be two farty!

Where do people in Antarctica go to get a haircut?

The brrrr-brrrr shop.

What did the French fish say
with his last breath?
Fin.
Eiffel over
in laughter!

Joke-Telling Tips!

- Know your audience
- Timing is everything
- Confidence is key
- Go out on a high note!

Glossary

fin
the French word for "finished" or "end." It often appears at the end of some classic foreign movies.

pun
a joke using a word that sounds like a different word or has another meaning. Examples from this book are "Pear-is" (Paris) and "ketchup" (catch up).

Index